3800 18 0031196 5

HIGH LIFE HIGHLAND

KT-417-423

HIGHLAND
LIBRARIES

WITHDRAWN

HIGH LIFE HIGHLAND LIBRARIES	
38001800311965	
BERTRAMS	24/07/2018
J 070.43	£13.99
JNF	

WHO? WHAT? WHY?

WHAT IS FAKE NEWS?

IZZI HOWELL

WAYLAND
www.waylandbooks.co.uk

First published in Great Britain in 2018 by Wayland

Copyright © Hodder and Stoughton Limited, 2018

All rights reserved.

ISBN 978 1 5263 0881 8
10 9 8 7 6 5 4 3 2 1

Wayland
An imprint of
Hachette Children's Group
Part of Hodder & Stoughton
Carmelite House
50 Victoria Embankment
London EC4Y 0DZ

An Hachette UK Company
www.hachette.co.uk
www. hachettechildrens.co.uk

A catalogue for this title is available from the British Library.

Printed in Malaysia.

MIX
Paper from
responsible sources
FSC® C104740

Produced for Wayland
by White-Thomson Publishing Ltd
www.wtpub.co.uk
Editor: Izzi Howell
Designer: Dan Prescott, Couper Street Type Co.

Picture acknowledgements:
Alamy: Dinendra Haria 13b and 20, Mark Kerrison 18, Everett Collection Inc 39, Juergen Hasenkopf 43; Getty: SSPL 5, blackred 7, tefan Rousseau - WPA Pool 9, NOEL CELIS/AFP 11, DANIEL LEAL-OLIVAS/AFP 13t, Jack Taylor 14, ALEXEY DRUZHININ/AFP 21, iodrakon 28, Michael E. Miller/The Washington Post 31, JEWEL SAMAD/AFP 33tr, MARK RALSTON/AFP 34, glegorly 36, Steve Debenport 42; National Parks Service 33tl; Shutterstock: sdecoret cover, Anthony Ricci title page and 45, Iryna Inshyna 3 and 24, Evan El-Amin 4, smereka 6, Lenscap Photography 8, Nice_Media_PRODUCTION 10, Everett Historical 15, Kebrun 16, Mr. Meijer 17, Rob Crandall 19, zorbital 22, Dean Drobot 25, sitthiphong 26, Jim Lambert 27, CK Foto 29, J. Louis Bryson 32 and 48, Sk Hasan Ali 33b, Ben Kailing 35, OVKNHR 38, Delpixel 40l, Ralf Siemieniec 40r, catwalker 44, Heidi Besen 47.

All graphic elements from Shutterstock.

Every attempt has been made to clear copyright. Should there be any inadvertent omission please apply to the publisher for rectification.

The website addresses (URLs) included in this book were valid at the time of going to press. However, it is possible that contents or addresses may have changed since the publication of this book. No responsibility for any such changes accepted by either the author or the publisher.

CONTENTS

WHAT IS FAKE NEWS?

Many people are talking about the problem of fake news stories at the moment. In fact, fake news is such an important recent topic that Collins Dictionary chose the term as their 'word of the year' for 2017. They define fake news as 'false, often sensational, information disseminated under the guise of news reporting'.

DEFINING FAKE NEWS

The term fake news is used to describe false, and often outrageous, information that is deliberately presented as a real news story. The creators of the story know that it is fake, but people who read and share the story may not.

KINDS OF FAKE NEWS

Some fake news stories are harmless and silly. For example, in November 2017, one story reported that a woman had trained 65 cats to steal jewellery from her neighbours. Many fake news stories are political. They are used to influence public opinion, create fear and damage the reputation of political figures or movements.

During the US election campaign in 2016, some fake news stories exaggerated Hillary Clinton's ill health. These stories were spread to try to convince people not to vote for Clinton. The writers of the stories wanted people to believe that she was too weak to be a good president.

4

HISTORY

Throughout history, there have always been people who have spread false or inaccurate information. However, the term 'fake news' wasn't used until the nineteenth century. The use of the term has been on the rise since 2015 and has increased by 365 per cent since 2016. We are using the term more and more as people become increasingly worried about the information they receive, particularly online.

Hoaxes, such as the Cottingley Fairies, could be seen as a type of fake news. In 1917, two young cousins in the UK took photos of paper fairies. The photos were printed in newspapers and many believed that they were real. In the 1980s, the cousins admitted that the photos were fake.

FAKE NEWS AND TRUMP

The increase in the use of the term 'fake news' can be linked to the rise of Donald Trump. During his election campaign and time as US president, Trump has shared various news reports that later turned out to be inaccurate. In fact, during his first year as president in 2017, it is estimated that he made 1,950 misleading or false claims. Trump also uses the term (and falsely claims to have invented it), to describe true and accurate news stories. These news stories often criticise his behaviour and views, present information that he doesn't agree with or challenge actions that he plans to take. Trump describes these stories as fake news to make it hard to know what is true and what is not.

WHERE DOES INFORMATION COME FROM?

To understand how fake news has entered our society, it is important to think about where information comes from. In the past, our information came from a few sources, such as books or newspapers. Today, there are millions of websites claiming to have the answer to almost any question. But how much of this information, on and offline, can be trusted?

FACTS

Facts are pieces of information that are proven to be true based on evidence. Generally, we need evidence from several sources to confirm that something is true. For example, we know that Queen Victoria was shorter than average height because we have photos and historical documents that confirm this. Facts are objective. This means that they are not based on feelings or opinions. Even if Queen Victoria believed she was tall, this would not change the fact that she was shorter than average.

BELIEFS

Beliefs are opinions that we hold. For example, some people believe that eating animals is wrong, while others do not see meat as a problem. Our family, our religion, our culture, our environment and our society influence our beliefs. Some beliefs can be supported by facts and evidence. A meat-eater might state that humans need protein as part of a balanced diet, and meat contains protein. A vegetarian might focus on the fact that some scientists have shown that animals can feel pain.

People who have opposing views about whether it is acceptable for humans to eat animals can offer facts to back up their opinions.

BELIEFS AND FACTS

Our beliefs may lead us to only focus on certain facts. It could be hard for a meat-eater to accept that animals feel pain. A vegetarian might not want to accept that meat can be part of a balanced diet. However, we must try to be open-minded about all facts, even if they go against what we believe.

EXPERIENCES AND FACTS

Our experiences can make it hard for us to believe facts. For example, someone who is unemployed and struggling for money may find it hard to believe the government if they say that unemployment is falling and the economy is doing well. Although these claims may be true, with evidence to support them, it can be hard to believe them if they do not match your own experience.

SOURCES OF FACTS

Facts can be found in traditional sources of information, such as books, newspapers, TV programmes and school curriculums. Most of these sources are controlled by media guidelines. If asked, the people who create the product must be able to show evidence for the information that they are presenting. They are responsible for any incorrect or misleading information that they share, and must correct it if proven wrong.

Books are a great source of information for homework or other projects.

ONLINE FACTS

Major newspapers and encyclopaedias have online presences, so that they can bring facts and information to a wider audience. Readers can expect these sources to be accurate and thoroughly checked. However, many websites and social media platforms are not checked for accuracy. They are not covered by media guidelines, so anyone can publish anything, even if there is no evidence to support it. Websites that collect information from across the Internet, such as search engines and social media sites, do not distinguish between fact-checked websites and websites that contain false information. For this reason, it can be hard to know if information found on the Internet is true or false.

IMPARTIALITY

Many traditional sources of information, such as newspapers, aim to be impartial (not supporting one point of view more than another). This means that they are careful to present different beliefs about facts and not show a preference. For example, if they are presenting information about a war, they will explain the different opinions of both sides.

POLITICAL BIAS

However, most newspapers and TV news programmes are not impartial. They may have a political bias that affects the way in which they present information. Even though media guidelines make sure that they present accurate facts, they may show their bias in other ways. A publication may deliberately leave out important details to change the meaning of a news story. News editors can also choose to only publish stories that suit their political beliefs. Some journalists use emotive language to influence people's reaction to a story. However, if any of this bias makes the information that they share untrue, they will have to remove it and publish an admission that it was wrong.

The UK headlines on the day before the EU membership referendum reveal the political leanings of different newspapers.

BALANCED VIEWS

When some newspapers and TV news programmes report on people's beliefs and interpretation of facts, they try to give everyone a voice and report on all sides of an argument. For example, during elections, news sources report on candidates from all main political parties. In theory, this is a good thing, as it makes news sources more balanced and impartial.

⬆ Leaders and members of different British political parties appear on a BBC debate. In the run-up to elections, the BBC lets all the leaders of major UK political parties explain their ideas.

TOO BALANCED?

Some sources of media have recently been criticised for giving a platform to people who do not have any facts to support their beliefs. For example, at least 97 per cent of scientists believe that human activity is responsible for recent global warming. This is confirmed by research and evidence. However, these scientists are sometimes, in the interests of balance, interviewed alongside climate change sceptics, who do not have evidence to support their beliefs. Appearing alongside scientists gives the sceptics' ideas equal weight. It also publicises their unproven views. People are likely to trust what they see in news reports, and so they may accept the sceptics' unproven beliefs as facts. Appearing alongside sceptics may also make experts and scientists seem less legitimate, as it might suggest that their proven views are opinions rather than facts.

> " Minority opinions and sceptical views should not be treated as if (they) were on an equal footing with the scientific consensus.
>
> • • • • • •
>
> **Fraser Steel, head of the BBC's Editorial Complaints Unit, 2014** "

WHAT IS PROPAGANDA?

Propaganda is information spread to influence public opinion. This information can be facts, half-truths, rumours or total lies. The goal of propaganda is to manipulate people's beliefs, rather than to educate them. Fake news stories that are deliberately designed to mislead people and influence their beliefs are examples of propaganda.

PROPAGANDA VS EDUCATION

Fact-checked, impartial sources of information educate people by...

- presenting various sides of an issue
- helping people to collect information for themselves
- encouraging people to come to their own conclusion.

Propaganda manipulates people by...

- distorting real evidence or providing false evidence
- presenting details in a way that plays with people's emotions, for example by making them angry
- making claims without any evidence
- encouraging people to trust their claims without any thought.

EARLY PROPAGANDA

Propaganda can be traced back thousands of years. The ancient Greeks studied rhetoric, the art of persuasive communication. They used flattery, emotive language, humour and other persuasive techniques to convince people they were telling the truth and to discredit other people's ideas.

TECHNOLOGY AND PROPAGANDA

New methods of communication have always been quickly adapted for propaganda. After the printing press was invented in the 1450s, printed pamphlets were used to spread propaganda. In the sixteenth century, Protestants used printed propaganda to help convince people that they should split from the Catholic Church. In the 1930s in Germany, the Nazi Party brought out a cheap, simple radio so that their supporters could listen to their political rallies and speeches at home, on the street and in cafes. From the mid-twentieth century onwards, propaganda films and TV programmes were produced.

ONLINE PROPAGANDA

Today, the Internet provides many opportunities for propaganda, including online fake news stories. Links to propaganda websites and propaganda images can be quickly and easily shared with a huge number of people via social media sites. These sites can be used for propaganda in more subtle ways too. In a 2017 study, 30 countries, including the Philippines and Turkey, were found to employ people to spread government propaganda and bully critics online. For other social media users, it is often unclear if these accounts truly support the government, or if they are just supporting them because they have been paid to do so.

In the Philippines, people have reported that they were being paid $10 USD a day to spread propaganda on social media in support of Rodrigo Duterte, the now-president, in the run up to the election in 2016.

USE OF PROPAGANDA TODAY

These days, every political group, government and
social movement has teams of people working out
how to spread their message through propaganda.
You will probably have seen propaganda posters,
fliers, articles and adverts in newspapers and on TV.
A range of persuasive techniques are used across
these different types of propaganda. Some techniques
are reasonable, while others are more controversial.

PROPAGANDA TECHNIQUES

- Suggesting that the ideas expressed reflect what 'the people' want
- Scapegoating (blaming someone for a bad situation that they have
  not caused)
- Using 'virtue words', such as peace, love, hope, freedom
- Including testimonials, sometimes out of context, to create a
  misleading effect
- Playing on group identity, by suggesting it is disloyal to a group/
  nation/religion to act in a certain way

PROPAGANDA AND BREXIT

During the Brexit campaign in the UK, both the Remain
and the Leave campaigns were accused of using propaganda
to influence public opinion. Critics of Remain alleged that
its campaigners were trying to convince people to stay in the
EU by creating fear that no one knew what would happen
economically or politically if the UK left. They played up
European identity, suggesting that it was disloyal for the UK
to leave Europe.

Critics of the Leave campaign alleged that its leaders
created fear about immigration and scapegoated the EU
for problems in the UK. They also stirred up nationalistic
pride, suggesting that the people of the UK should consider
themselves British, rather than European.

EXAMPLES OF BREXIT PROPAGANDA

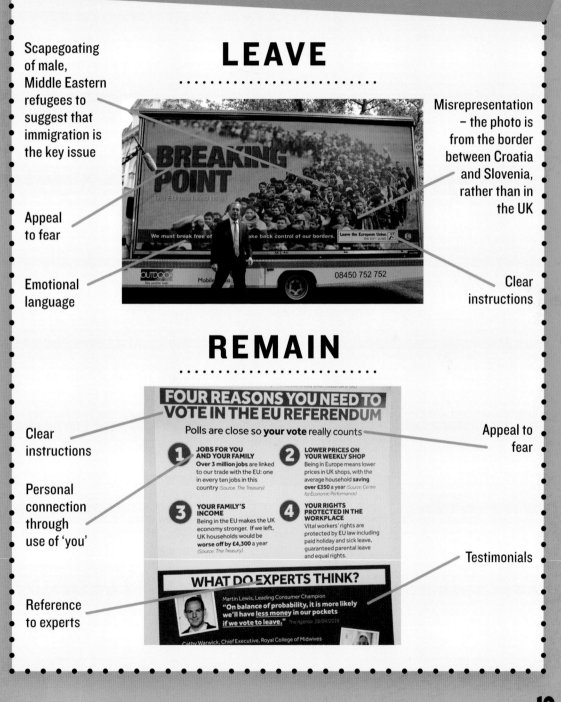

LEAVE

Scapegoating of male, Middle Eastern refugees to suggest that immigration is the key issue

Appeal to fear

Emotional language

Misrepresentation – the photo is from the border between Croatia and Slovenia, rather than in the UK

Clear instructions

REMAIN

Clear instructions

Personal connection through use of 'you'

Reference to experts

Appeal to fear

Testimonials

IS PROPAGANDA FAKE NEWS?

The most extreme forms of propaganda can be considered fake news. If propaganda contains incorrect information, forged images and false claims, it fits the definition of fake news (see page 4). Propaganda can also mislead people and seek to convince them with false information, even if it technically sticks to the facts (see panel).

THE LEAVE BREXIT BUS

The Leave campaign was heavily criticised for misleading people with its use of data, after they claimed that if the UK left the EU, £350 million a week could go to the NHS (National Health Service) rather than the EU. The figure itself was misleading, as it failed to mention that the UK also received money from the EU. The claim also made many people believe that the money *would* go to the NHS, when in fact, they were only suggesting that it *could*. As a result, many people were convinced by false information, just as if they had read a fake news story.

The Leave campaign posted their claims on a bus that was driven around the UK, spreading their message.

We send the EU **£350 million** a week let's fund our **NHS** instead Vote Leave

Let's take back control

66

Would we have won without £350m/NHS? All our research and the close result strongly suggests No.

. . . . . .

Dominic Cummings, the campaign director for the Leave Campaign explains why they were successful in a newspaper article in January 2017

99

DANGER OF PROPAGANDA

In some countries, such as the UK, propaganda is controlled. Claims have to be proven with evidence. The amount of money that political parties spend on advertising and propaganda is limited. This means that fake news propaganda from the main political parties is less common. However, there are some places in the world that do not have these controls. There, people can spread hateful false propaganda with no restrictions. This misinformation can lead to prejudice, violence and even war. Anti-Jewish propaganda was very important to the rise of the Nazi Party in Germany in the 1930s. In Rwanda, hateful media, particularly radio programmes, encouraged people from the Hutu ethnic group to kill people from the Tutsi ethnic group. This contributed to the genocide of over 800,000 Tutsis and moderate Hutus in 1994.

 This Nazi poster accuses Jewish people of starting the Second World War and making it last longer.

HOW CAN WE SOLVE THE PROBLEM OF PROPAGANDA?

As long as propaganda is based on evidence, it isn't necessarily a problem. It is not wrong or illegal to try to persuade someone else. However, as with news stories, it is important to look at propaganda critically and check that its claims are accurate. See pages 36–41 for tips on how to spot fake news or propaganda.

WHY CREATE FAKE NEWS?

People create fake news stories for different reasons. The creators of silly fake news stories about celebrities and animals are usually doing it for different reasons than the creators of fake political news stories. But what exactly motivates people to create fake news stories?

CLICKBAIT

Clickbait is a term used to describe things that attract people's attention online and make them want to find out more. They often don't reveal all of the information, so visitors are tempted to click on the link and find out more. When people visit the website, it makes money for the website creators through advertising programs.

Would you want to click on this link? Why?

➤

Find out how dolphins can read your mind!

FAKE NEWS AS CLICKBAIT

Fake news stories work well as clickbait because they are outrageous. People are sucked in and want to find out more. They are often ridiculous stories about celebrities or too-good-to-be true claims about how to make money, but they can also be political. However, the main goal of these fake news stories is to earn money for the creators.

HOAXES

Some people consider it funny to 'trick' people with fake news stories. They publish ridiculous stories to see who falls for them. Many people will realise that these posts are untrue, but may share them anyway, as they find them funny. Some people, though, will be fooled.

HOAX TRAPS

Posting silly hoaxes can be a way of damaging a person's reputation. If someone falls for a hoax and shares it, they can easily be accused of being unintelligent or of deliberately spreading lies. For example, in 2014, Donald Trump was tricked into retweeting a photo of two serial killers, after someone claimed it was a photo of his parents celebrating their birthday. After Donald Trump did this, some people criticised him.

In January 2018, over 25,000 people retweeted a tweet that falsely claimed that President Trump wanted to watch 'a gorilla channel' that showed gorillas 24 hours a day.

LACK OF EVIDENCE

In most cases, people create political fake news when they have little or no evidence that supports their opinions. Usually, when we believe something, it is because we have evidence that supports our belief. If we want to persuade others to agree with our opinions, we share the evidence with them. Therefore, if a group makes a claim with no evidence, or with false evidence, we can assume that they do not have any proof to back up their beliefs.

INFLUENCE PUBLIC OPINION

Many fake news stories play on fears or prejudices that people may already hold. They often stir up fear or distrust of minority groups, such as people from different countries or ethnic groups, immigrants, disabled people or the LGBT community. The publishers of these stories benefit in some way from people holding prejudiced beliefs. For example, they may want to limit immigration or deny disabled people economic support.

These people publish this type of fake news story because they know that prejudiced people will want to look at information that confirms their existing beliefs. This makes their beliefs grow stronger. These stories may also convince people who don't already hold prejudices. After seeing many fake news stories reporting fear and hatred, they may be persuaded there is actually some truth in the stories.

Anti-racism protestors take part in the March Against Racism in London in March 2017 to try to stop prejudice and racism, including that caused by fake news.

DISCREDIT IDEAS

Spreading fake news stories has proven to be an effective way of discrediting ideas and political groups. Even if the stories are later proven to be untrue, it can be hard to escape them. Before the EU membership referendum, the pro-Leave campaign created fear about staying in the EU. One of their stories reported that if the UK stayed in the EU, five million more European immigrants could come to the UK by 2030. This statistic is based on possible plans to let more eastern European countries join the EU, which are not yet final. However, worry about immigration was one of the main reasons why people voted to leave the EU.

DISCREDIT PEOPLE

Some public figures have had their reputations permanently damaged by fake news stories. For example, former US president, George W. Bush, gained a reputation for being not very bright. This was linked to a range of fake news stories published about him, such as that he has the lowest IQ of any president and that once he didn't realise he was reading a book upside down. These stories are false, but both damaged the public's perception of him. Some people use this technique as a way of fighting against their political rivals.

Fake news stories damaged George W. Bush's reputation.

WHO IS CREATING FAKE NEWS?

A wide range of different groups, governments and individuals create fake news stories. Some support right-wing politics, while some are left-wing. Others aren't motivated by politics and just create fake news stories in exchange for money.

RIGHT-WING/LEFT-WING

It may seem that fake news is mainly created by people with right-wing politics, as many fake news stories do support right-wing views. Of the 20 most-seen fake news stories in the period of the 2016 US election, all but three were pro-Donald Trump or anti-Hillary Clinton. These included false information, such as that Hillary Clinton sold weapons to Islamic State and that the Pope was a Trump supporter. Anti-immigration fake news stories regularly appear, spreading false information about links between immigration and crime. However, there are also left-wing groups creating fake news stories. One of these stories claimed that a young child was handcuffed at an airport because of Trump's travel ban on visitors from certain Muslim countries, which was later proven to be untrue.

In March 2017, the right-wing Sun newspaper in the UK published a story claiming that the Queen supported Brexit. The Queen later placed an official complaint about the story's accuracy.

NEWS WEBSITES

One of the biggest websites that allegedly posts deliberately misleading news stories is Breitbart, a source of right-wing news and opinion. Breitbart played a significant role in spreading the fake news story that Barack Obama was a Muslim born in Kenya. He is actually a Christian who was born in the US state of Hawaii. There are also thousands of other small websites run by individuals who publish fake news stories disguised as real news articles. They often pay for adverts on social media in the hope that their message will be shared.

Russia Today is a TV news channel and website controlled by the Russian government that claims to provide 'an alternative perspective on major global events', but has been accused by the media of supplying misleading and inaccurate information. It looks very similar to traditional news channels, so many viewers may not realise that some of its content may not be true.

GOVERNMENTS

In most democratic countries with a free press, governments spread controlled propaganda, but not fake news. Media guidelines require that they provide evidence to support any claims. In other countries, governments widely spread misleading information and fake news. In North Korea, many ridiculous reports are regularly shared, such as that former leader Kim Jong-il wrote 1,500 books in three years.

In 2011, some people doubted official reports that Vladimir Putin, the Russian prime minister, had discovered two ancient Greek jugs while diving. The urns were suspiciously clean, and found in a location previously checked by archaeologists.

OTHER COUNTRIES

We are starting to learn more and more about how countries are manipulating foreign politics through fake news. Russian citizens have been formally accused of spreading fake news in the run-up to the 2016 US election to help Donald Trump's campaign. Between January 2015 and August 2017, it is estimated that more than 146m Facebook users may have seen Russian misinformation on the site.

In Macedonia, groups of people are employed to create fake news for money. They do not have any personal reason to create these stories – they just benefit by being paid for them. During the US election campaign, at least 100 pro-Trump websites sharing fake news were traced to one Macedonian town.

Many pro-Trump websites sharing fake news have been traced to the Macedonian town of Veles.

> " The Americans loved our stories and we make money from them...who cares if they are true or false?
>
> • • • • • •
>
> **An anonymous 19-year-old Macedonian fake news creator, 2016** "

EXTREMIST GROUPS

Extremist groups such as fascists, terrorists and far-right hate groups regularly share fake news online. White nationalists post fake news stories suggesting that white people are at risk from people of other races. They want to create fear and strengthen the beliefs of people who already hold prejudices. The extremist Islamist terrorist group Islamic State tries to find new members by sharing propaganda videos and articles that present them as powerful and successful.

BOTS

Bots are computer programs that talk and act like humans. They play an important role in the spreading of fake news. There are thousands of bots online that are programmed to post links to fake news articles and to comment on social media platforms with false information. During the 2016 US election campaign, it is thought that bots generated one in five political posts. Many Internet users will not be able to tell the difference between a bot account and a human account.

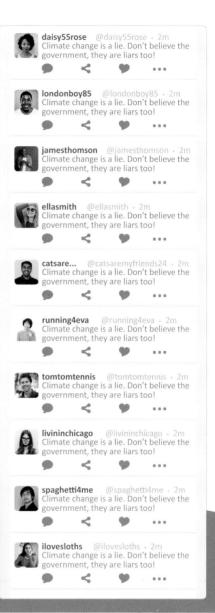

➡️

Bots accounts may look real, with a realistic name and profile photo. However, they may do suspicious things, such as post exactly the same wording multiple times.

GOING VIRAL

Bots can be used to make a fake news post or video 'go viral'. If thousands of bots are programmed to interact with a post, it will be placed higher in the algorithm (computer program) that decides what we see (see page 26). This makes it more likely that other people will see it.

WHY DO WE SEE FAKE NEWS ON SOCIAL MEDIA?

Social media sites are filled with information and news. As we scroll down, we can see links to articles, personal posts about news stories and other people's responses to posts. It is quick and easy to use social media to get up-to-date on current affairs, so it isn't surprising that two thirds of adults in the USA get at least some of their news from social media. However, some of the news posted on social media is fake news. But why are fake news stories so successful on social media and why do we see these stories on our feeds?

ATTENTION

The key to social media success is being able to grab people's attention. There is so much information online that people find it very hard to focus on one thing. Social media feeds constantly update themselves, displaying new content with every page refresh. But social media companies and content creators need to capture people's attention and get them to engage in order to make money. There are different strategies that can be used to get people's attention on social media.

The average person spends two hours a day on social media. ↑

TOO FAST TO THINK

Our short attention span online benefits the creators of fake news. We spend so little time looking at their content that we are unlikely to think about it critically or investigate the evidence or claims that they make.

OUTRAGE

One of the best ways to capture people's attention is through outrage. Shocking headlines stand out against other content. People are also likely to engage with provocative posts – they comment angrily on the post, share it with others and respond to other people's comments, becoming more and more worked up as they do so. For this reason, fake news stories are often deliberately outrageous; making ridiculous and offensive claims that will encourage people to react to them.

APPEAL OF FAKE NEWS STORIES

IN THE FINAL THREE MONTHS OF THE US ELECTION CAMPAIGN IN 2016:

20 TOP-PERFORMING FAKE NEWS STORIES FROM HOAX SITES GENERATED

8,711,000

SHARES, REACTIONS AND COMMENTS ON FACEBOOK

20 TOP-PERFORMING NEWS STORIES FROM MAJOR NEWS WEBSITES GENERATED

7,367,000

SHARES, REACTIONS AND COMMENTS ON FACEBOOK

ANGER SPREADS QUICKLY

A 2014 study in China found that social media users reacted fastest to posts that make them feel angry. They reacted much more quickly to these posts than to posts that made them feel happy or sad. Angry posts are also likely to go viral. When users shared angry posts, it made their followers equally furious, spreading the angry content across the social media network.

ALGORITHMS

Computer programs called algorithms on social media sites choose which information to show you, ranging from adverts to posts and links shared by contacts. They favour posts that many people have interacted with. People interact a lot with fake news posts, sometimes more than with real news posts. Fake news creators also pay for bots or real people to interact with the fake news stories that they create. This boosts the position of posts in the algorithms and makes other people more likely to see them on social media.

The more 'likes' or reactions a post has on Facebook, the more likely it is that other people will see it.

LIKES AND DISLIKES

Algorithms are also heavily favoured towards content that you are personally likely to pay attention to and interact with. The algorithms identify users' likes and dislikes by looking at data that users upload, such as posts, likes, shares, groups and contacts. They choose only to show you content that reflects your likes and interests. So, as soon as you start interacting with fake news posts, you are likely to see more and more of them.

ECHO CHAMBERS

The use of algorithms means that social media users usually only see content that confirms their existing likes, dislikes and opinions. This is described as an echo chamber. If we only see information that supports our current views, it is likely to make them stronger. It also makes people more vulnerable to fake news. If we are used to believing everything that we see on social media, it makes it harder for us to think critically about what we read, even if it seems outrageous.

> "You are basically indoctrinating yourself with your own views and you don't even know it. You don't know what you see is the part of the picture that reflects what you want to see, not the whole picture.
>
> **Eli Parisier, the author of *The Filter Bubble*, 2011**"

UNFOLLOWING

We often tend to 'unfollow' anyone that does not share our views on social media. This reduces the range of different beliefs that we are exposed to even further. For those who are already getting most of their information from fake news sites through social media, it is very unlikely that they will come into contact with real news reports in a social media echo chamber.

ECHO CHAMBER CONFUSION

Echo chambers can lead to a biased view of current affairs. For example, many Remain supporters were shocked by the result of the Brexit vote (see pages 12–13), as they were sure that their campaign would win. In the run up to the vote, their social media platforms had been filled with posts from others that supported the Remain campaign. After the vote, they were shocked to discover that nearly 52 per cent of the country did not feel the same way that they did.

Although people publically showed their support for Donald Trump before the election, many Democrats were surprised by the election results. Their social media echo chamber had stopped them from seeing messages supporting Trump online.

SHARING IS EASY

It is incredibly easy for social media users to share links and posts. It just takes one click to share something with hundreds of followers. Every person that reposts the original post increases the audience even further. This means very little effort is needed to spread fake news on social media. It just takes a few malicious or misled people to spread false information across thousands of accounts.

ATTENTION FROM FRIENDS

It is not just online businesses and social media platforms that are addicted to online attention. Social media users also want their friends and social media followers to pay them attention by liking and sharing their posts and leaving comments. They may, even without realising, prefer to post shocking or outrageous content (including fake news stories), as these posts tend to get a more dramatic response and more attention from their followers.
This helps to spread fake news stories.

A 2016 study found that receiving likes on social media activated the same part of teenagers' brains as winning money.

PLAYING JOURNALIST

Some social media users like to play the role of journalist online. They put news stories in their own words and share their reports with the world. Unlike real journalists, they do not try to verify the stories they are sharing and there are no consequences for sharing false information. So, it is relatively easy for people to accidentally or deliberately share false information. For this reason, we should be cautious about getting our news from individuals on social media. Fake news content from individual social media accounts is much harder to trace and remove than stories from fake news websites, as it can come from so many different sources.

On 9 November 2016, one Twitter user posted a tweet and photo, reporting that he had seen coaches used to bring paid protesters to join in anti-Trump demonstrations. His tweet quickly went viral, being shared 16,000 times on Twitter and 350,000 times on Facebook. However, his reports were not accurate. The coaches were actually used for a company conference.

> " I don't have time to fact-check everything that I put out there, especially when I don't think it's going out there for wide consumption.
>
> . . . . . .
>
> **The Twitter user who posted the coach tweet** "

ONLINE IDENTITY

Our social media profiles have become a huge part of who we are. What we post and comment on online affects other people's opinions of us. So some people think it's important to make posts that reflect their beliefs, so that other people will see them. Our desire to define ourselves online can get in the way of the truth. Some people care more about what posting a story says about them, than about whether the story is true. This may result in them sharing fake news stories.

WHAT ARE THE DANGERS OF FAKE NEWS?

Fake news stories are usually outrageous or scandalous. They are designed to make us react emotionally, as this means that we are more likely to respond or share them with other people. Our emotional response to these fake stories can make them very powerful.

MISINFORMED DECISIONS

We use evidence to help us make informed decisions about what to think and how to behave. However, if people accept misleading or incorrect information from fake news stories, their beliefs and decisions will be misinformed. This may lead to them making poor choices or decisions that they may later regret.

> " I personally voted Leave believing these lies, and I regret it more than anything, I feel genuinely robbed of my vote.
>
> • • • • • •
>
> **One Leave voter who regretted voting for Brexit, quoted in the *Independent* newspaper in June 2016** "

INCREASING PREJUDICES

As we've seen, fake news stories often play on prejudices or fears that people may already hold. Every time that a fake news story presents a negative story or a false stereotype about a certain group of people, it is likely to confirm the opinions of prejudiced people. They feel more confident that their prejudiced beliefs are justified, as they have seen supporting evidence 'in the news'. Over time, they may start to openly express their hatred because they now feel that their views are acceptable and that other people agree with them. This can lead to hate crimes.

FAKE NEWS STORIES ABOUT MUSLIMS

- Muslims have forced Burger King to stop selling bacon.
- A Muslim mayor banned his town from celebrating Christmas.
- A group of Muslims attacked some men in a pub for drinking beer.

The creators of these clickbait stories hope that people who are already prejudiced against Muslims will feel outraged when they read them and will want to share them. In this way, they will pass their prejudice on to others.

EXTREME REACTIONS

Fake news stories can lead people to take extreme action. After reading shocking or outrageous claims, they may feel frustrated that no one is reacting or trying to solve the problem. They are convinced that it is a real problem, although it is actually false. A few people may try to deal with the supposed problem themselves. For example, in December 2016, one man brought a gun to a pizza shop in Washington DC, USA, and threatened an employee after reading a fake news story about Hillary Clinton and her campaign chief abusing children there. This fake news story is known as Pizzagate. In the five weeks before this event, people had tweeted about Pizzagate around 1.4 million times.

WHO WAS TWEETING ABOUT PIZZAGATE?

. . . .

RUSSIAN-LINKED ACCOUNTS

BOTS

A 50-YEAR-OLD GRANDMOTHER FROM PENNSYLVANIA, WHO TWEETED ABOUT THE STORY MORE THAN 4,000 TIMES IN FIVE WEEKS

ACCOUNTS FOLLOWED BY 66 DIFFERENT TRUMP CAMPAIGN ADVISERS AND STAFF MEMBERS

A few people still believe the Pizzagate rumours. They protested outside the White House in Washington DC on 25 March 2017, calling for an investigation.

WHY ARE TRUE STORIES DESCRIBED AS FAKE NEWS?

A few people, including, famously, Donald Trump, accuse real news of being fake news. This is a way of shutting down critical, while accurate, reports and is part of a campaign against the so-called 'mainstream' media. In doing this, they aim to shake people's confidence and trust in reporting by the mainstream media.

TRUMP AND THE MEDIA

Trump regularly describes news coverage that is critical of him as fake news. He often makes these claims on his personal Twitter account. Some of the things he has accused of being 'fake news' include coverage from all the main media outlets except for Fox News, reports that link him and his electoral campaign to Russia and criticisms that he hasn't done enough to help Puerto Rico recover from Hurricane Maria in 2017.

> " I have a running war with the media. They are among the most dishonest human beings on Earth.
>
> • • • • • •
>
> **Trump in a speech at the CIA headquarters in January 2017** "

Generally speaking, such criticisms are based on evidence. For example, many Puerto Ricans still did not have electricity or clean water months after the hurricane, as aid from the USA had not arrived or had not been distributed. Trump rarely responds to these reports with valid evidence that proves that the criticisms are untrue. Instead, he ends the discussion by calling them 'fake news'. Some commentators have suggested that he shuts down the discussion because the criticisms are true.

➡ Campaigners protest against Trump at a march in Toronto, Canada, in January 2018.

MY OPINION TRUMPS YOUR FACTS
MrTrumphead.com

TRUMP'S INAUGURATION

In January 2017, there was some disagreement over the size of the crowd at Trump's inauguration. After journalists reported that Trump's inauguration had not had a high attendance compared to previous inaugurations, Trump's press secretary accused them of spreading fake news. He claimed that the crowd at Trump's inauguration had been "the largest audience ever to witness an inauguration, period, both in person and around the globe".

Aerial photos taken at Trump's (left) and Obama's 2009 inauguration ceremonies provide evidence to support the journalists' claims of the crowd size.

FAKE NEWS IN BURMA

In Burma, the government is denying proven reports of soldiers from the Burmese army attacking and killing people from the Rohingya minority and claiming that the reports are fake news. It has been reported that the government is also spreading fake images themselves and claiming that they came from the Rohingya, in an attempt to discredit the accurate reports.

Rohingya refugees wait to cross the border between Burma and Bangladesh in October 2017. So far, around 870,000 Rohingya have been forced to leave Burma to avoid violence.

33

REMOVING THE MEDIA

As well as his campaign to discredit journalists as suppliers of 'fake news', Trump has banned journalists from many major news providers from White House briefings. By removing the media, he has reduced the number of evidence-based sources reporting on these events. This leaves Trump, and other potentially biased and misleading media outlets, as the only sources of information. People are only told what the government wants them to know, which makes them vulnerable to false information and propaganda. This is why throughout history many dictators and oppressive regimes have tried to censor the press, as it is one of the most successful ways of controlling people.

ANGER AT PEOPLE IN CHARGE

Many of Trump's supporters are people who feel angry about the gap between the rich and the poor growing bigger. They feel as if past politicians tricked them when they said that they would help. This has made them lose trust in those who are in charge. They also consider the media, and the experts that they call on for their views, as part of the problem. They don't believe that the media could be on their side. Therefore, they may reject the media's claims, and instead turn to alternative news sites that often share false or misleading information.

A Trump supporter accuses the US news network CNN of lying in October 2016.

TRUMP
MAKE AMERICA GREAT AGAIN!

Paid for by Donald J. Trump for President, Inc.

CNN
¡Lies!
¡Lies!
¡Lies!
33,000
DELETED
EMAILS

POST–TRUTH

It is easy to become overwhelmed trying to work out which reports that look true are actually fake, and which reports being called fake are actually true. People can start to give up on being informed, as it is too difficult to decide what the truth is. If people can't depend on the objective truth, they may base their view of reality on opinions instead. They claim that something is true because they want it to be, regardless of whether or not it happened. This world-view is described as 'post-truth', in which facts matter less to people than personal beliefs.

THE DANGER OF POST–TRUTH THINKING

It is very dangerous for people to care more about beliefs than evidence. If we stop paying attention to facts, our beliefs can be misguided and inaccurate. If we act on these beliefs, we could harm ourselves and others. It would be also easy for people with malicious intentions to manipulate us and get us to do what they want.

> "
> I stand by the idea that it's a terror attack. I don't shy away from that. It's my personal opinion.
>
> • • • • • •
>
> **The controversial public figure Katie Hopkins, speaking about a car crash in London that she had described as a terror attack on Twitter in October 2017**
> "

A protestor marches to raise awareness of the importance of evidence and truth in science at the March for Science in Texas on 22 April 2017.

35

HOW CAN WE SPOT FAKE NEWS?

We often trust that anything we read is accurate and true. However, as we've seen, this is not always the case, especially on the Internet. There are various strategies that we can use to help us tell the difference between real news and fake news.

READ THE WHOLE STORY

Headlines can be deliberately misleading to grab people's attention. For example, in 2013, one UK newspaper ran a story with the headline "Air pollution now leading cause of lung cancer". However, in the article, it is revealed that air pollution is only the leading environmental cause. Other causes, such as smoking, are still much more likely to cause lung cancer than air pollution. A reader who only read the headline would not have this information. For this reason, it's important to read the whole article, rather than just the title.

→ It's important to read past the headline to get information from the main part of the article. This stops us being misled by inaccurate headlines. Photos can also be misleading or fake (see page 39).

BREAKING NEWS

ALIEN LIFE FOUND

Lorem ipsum dolor sit amet, consectetur adipiscing elit, sed do eiusmod tempor incididunt ut labore et dolore magna aliqua. Ut enim ad minim veniam, quis nostrud exercitation ullamco laboris nisi ut aliquip ex ea commodo consequat. Duis aute irure dolor in reprehenderit in voluptate velit esse cillum dolore eu fugiat nulla pariatur. Excepteur sint occaecat cupidatat non proident, sunt in culpa qui officia deserunt mollit anim id est laborum.

RESEARCH THE SOURCE

If you are reading a story on a news website, it is worth looking around the website to see if it looks like a real news organisation. Check if it has contact details or information about staff members. Many fake news websites do not contain this information.

Some websites with fake news stories are open about the fact that their stories are untrue. They might describe themselves as 'fantasy news'. However, these warnings are often well hidden on the website. Other websites post satirical stories that make a statement about current events using humour. They may look real, but they are actually joke stories and do not contain true information.

RESEARCH THE AUTHOR

Real news articles should have a byline that states who wrote the article. If there isn't a byline, it might be a sign that the article is not accurate. If there is a byline, do some research into the writer. Look at how they present themselves on social media and at other articles that they have written and other news organisations that they may have worked for.

Look for the byline when reading an article online.

CHECK THE DATE

Some fake news articles contain details of real events from the past. However, the writer twists the story to make it look as if the past events have recently happened, making the news story inaccurate. For example, in August 2015, the Ford car company moved its truck production factories from Mexico to Ohio, USA. However, some fake news websites reported that the company had moved in November 2016 as a result of Trump's election win. This false news story was designed to suggest that Trump's win was helping create jobs in the USA.

 Workers at a Ford factory in Turkey. Ford has car factories across the world.

CHECK THE SOURCES

If a newspaper or website makes a claim, they should provide supporting evidence, such as a date and context for a quotation or research for statistics. Readers should be suspicious if there are no sources for a claim. If there is evidence, check that it does support the claim made in the article.

It is also worth checking evidence and statistics to make sure that they are actually correct. In November 2015, Donald Trump retweeted a graphic that listed US crime statistics according to race. The graphic listed the source of the statistics as "Crime Statistics Bureau – San Francisco", which does not exist. The statistics were incorrect, but the graphic was designed to look authentic so that people would believe its false claims that white people were at risk from black people.

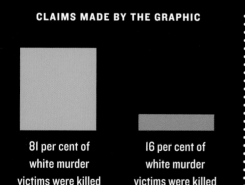

CLAIMS MADE BY THE GRAPHIC

81 per cent of white murder victims were killed by black people

16 per cent of white murder victims were killed by white people

CORRECT STATISTICS FROM PUBLICALLY AVAILABLE FBI REPORTS

14.8 per cent of white murder victims were killed by black people

82.4 per cent were killed by white people.

CHECK IMAGES

It is also worth checking images. Some articles are illustrated using images that come from different news stories. This can be misleading. You can use the Search by image feature in Google Images to check all the places that an image appears online. If the image was originally used to illustrate a different story, the image is probably not an accurate addition to the news story. Images can also be manipulated to add in different backgrounds and figures, or to remove things altogether.

1.

Google images

Search by image

2.

Google images

Search by image   ✕

Paste image URL   Upload an image

Search by image

These are the two steps to searching by an image in Google Images.

This computer-generated image from the 2004 film *The Day After Tomorrow* was spread on social media in 2012 by people claiming it showed Hurricane Sandy hitting New York.

CHECK OTHER PUBLICATIONS

It can be useful to see if a news story is reported in other places. If a story is reported in several major newspapers, it can be a sign that the story is true. This is because these publications are held to high journalistic guidelines and standards and are likely to have checked that it is true. It can be interesting to compare how each publication presents the same story. Which details are the same and what is different? Does the political bias of the publication (see page 8) affect the way in which it presents the story? It can help to look at different publications to establish the basic facts of what happened and separate them from any opinions expressed, and then come to your own conclusion.

CONSULT A FACT-CHECKING WEBSITE

Websites such as FactCheck.org, Snopes.com, the *Washington Post* Fact Checker and PolitiFact.com specialise in checking news stories to see if they are true or false. If you have doubts about a story that you read, you can check the story on one of these websites to find out more information.

Snopes.com also debunks false fun facts. For example, some websites have been claiming that the yolks of flamingo eggs are bright pink. This is untrue – their yolks are yellowy-orange like chicken egg yolks.

CHECK YOUR BIASES

It can be hard to look critically at information that goes against our views. We tend to trust information that confirms what we already believe, rather than new information that goes against what we believe. This is known as confirmation bias.

CONFIRMATION BIAS

Confirmation bias can make us vulnerable to fake news stories, if they confirm something that we already believe to be true. It's easy to be sceptical towards articles that go against what we believe, but we must also check articles that we agree with. Go through the steps listed in this chapter to make sure that an article is accurate.

Confirmation bias can also make it difficult for us to change our minds. Even if we are shown evidence that disproves our current beliefs, we might ignore it or look for ways to criticise it, so that we can keep on thinking in the same way.

1

Test your confirmation bias. Cover the panel on the right and read the following statements.

1. Fortune cookies were invented in China.
2. Vikings had horns on their helmets.
3. Goldfish have a memory of a few seconds.
4. A penny dropped from the top of the Empire State Building will kill a person on the ground below.

Have you heard any of these statements before? Which do you think are true?

2

They are all false statements.

1. Fortune cookies were invented in Japan and brought to the USA by Japanese immigrants.
2. There is no evidence that Vikings wore horned helmets.
3. The memory of goldfish is much longer than a few seconds, probably lasting for months.
4. The force of a penny dropped from the top of the Empire State Building is not strong enough to break someone's skull and kill them.

Does this evidence help you to change your mind?

41

HOW CAN WE STOP FAKE NEWS?

It may seem very difficult to stop the spread of fake news. However, there are several strategies that will help to reduce the amount of fake news online and to limit the affect that it has on people. Schools, governments, social media users and the creators of social media platforms all have a role to play.

EDUCATION

One of the simplest ways to stop the spread of fake news is to raise awareness of the issue. At school, younger children should be taught how to think critically about the information they are given. They should learn how to check sources and provide evidence for their beliefs. As they become older, this will help them to work out the difference between accurate and fake news.

It's important that students who use the Internet at school and at home know how to avoid fake news stories.

LAWS

Some people think that governments should apply the laws that control traditional media to all news websites. If these laws applied, creators of fake news websites could be forced to correct or remove incorrect reports. They could also be taken to court for publishing untrue damaging information about other people or political groups. If they encouraged prejudice or hatred, they could face time in jail.

POLICING THE INTERNET

The size of the Internet and the number of websites makes fake news very hard to police. However, it is possible. In China, more than two million moderators constantly check the Internet, censoring content and deleting anything that the Chinese government does not want its citizens to see. Across the world, moderators keep control over news website comment sections, deleting offensive remarks. A similar system could be used to remove fake news stories. However, if online news websites were to be regulated and controlled, commentators point out that an impartial Internet control board would need to be in charge of the content. It would not be appropriate for governments to control what is shown. At best, governments can be impartial and may use propaganda techniques to influence people through information. At worst, they spread fake news stories themselves.

In Qatar, the Internet providers block websites that contain material that the government considers inappropriate.

> **Tim Berners-Lee, the creator of the World Wide Web, does not believe that the content of websites should be controlled.**
>
> We must push back against misinformation by encouraging gatekeepers such as Google and Facebook to continue their efforts to combat the problem, while avoiding the creation of any central bodies to decide what is "true" or not.
>
> **Tim Berners-Lee, an open letter on his website, 12 March 2017**

CONTROLLING SOCIAL MEDIA

It would be even harder to control the spread of fake news on social media platforms, as there are so many users constantly publishing information. However, a few high profile cases in which misinformation was published online have already been taken to court. In the UK, the media personality Katie Hopkins had to pay £24,000 in damages and more than £100,000 in legal fees after posting tweets suggesting that the writer Jack Monroe approved of the defacing of a war memorial, with no evidence for her claim. From October 2017, Germany has required social media companies to take down fake news and hate speech such as Holocaust denial within 24 hours, or they will face fines of up to €50 million.

TECHNOLOGICAL SOLUTIONS

There are many ways in which social media platforms could adjust their websites to stop the spread of fake news.

- Cut down on bots that spread fake news stories
- Change algorithms to include a wider mix of material
- Add warnings to shared links that come from websites known to publish fake news
- Add pop ups that appear when people try to share links from fake news websites, checking if they want to share possibly false information
- Take down links to fake news content

> The world feels anxious and divided, and Facebook has a lot of work to do – whether it's protecting our community from abuse and hate, defending against interference by nation states, or making sure that time spent on Facebook is time well spent.
>
> **Mark Zuckerberg on a post on his personal Facebook page, 4 January 2018**

Mark Zuckerberg, the creator of Facebook, is starting to take the threat of fake news on social media seriously. Some people consider that social media platforms, such as Facebook, should take responsibility for and remove any fake news that is posted and shared on their site.

> After Donald Trump retweeted videos with an inaccurate, anti-Muslim message, Twitter released a statement saying it was not going to take them down, explaining:
>
> • • • • • •
>
> To help ensure people have an opportunity to see every side of an issue, there may be the rare occasion when we allow controversial content or behaviour which may otherwise violate our rules to remain on our service because we believe there is a legitimate public interest in its availability.

REDIRECTION

One idea to combat the effect of fake news is to redirect people to calming content after they have engaged with negative or shocking stories. The aim is to stop them from getting worked up and make it less likely that they will interact with more outrageous fake news stories. Youtube has already started to do this. Viewers of extremist Islamist videos are redirected to videos that show the opposite view.

OUR RESPONSIBILITY

We all have a personal responsibility to stop the spread of fake news. We can check the content of what we read and share (see pages 36–41) and encourage others to do the same. We can look for evidence to support our beliefs, and if there is none, be open to changing our mind. We can think critically about claims made by politicians and political groups, and challenge unproven statements. The truth is extremely important – if people stop caring about what is true, it will be much easier for others to manipulate them for their own ends.

A protestor carries a pro-truth sign at the March for Truth in Rhode Island, USA on 3 June 2017.

GLOSSARY

ALGORITHM – a computer program that decides what is shown on a website

BIAS – unfairly supporting or opposing an idea or person because of your personal beliefs

BOT – an automatic computer program that makes posts online and interacts on social media

CENSOR – to remove information that you do not want other people to see

CLICKBAIT – something on the Internet that is designed to attract people's attention so that they click on it

CONFIRM – to say or show that something is true

CONFIRMATION BIAS – the way in which we are more likely to trust information that agrees with our existing beliefs

CRITICALLY – if you think critically about something, you have thought carefully about what is right and what is wrong about it

DISCREDIT – to make someone stop respecting someone or believing something

ECHO CHAMBER – the state of only seeing information that we agree with and that confirms what we already believe

EMOTIVE – describes something that causes strong emotions

EVIDENCE – something presented in support of a claim that something is true

EXTREMIST – describes beliefs that are so strong that most people think they are unreasonable and unacceptable

HOAX – a trick in which someone tries to make someone believe something untrue

IMPARTIAL – not supporting one person, group or idea more than another

MANIPULATE – to control someone in a clever way that makes them do what you want them to do

MEDIA GUIDELINES – rules about presenting factual news stories that printed newspapers and some TV new channels have to follow

MISLEADING – describes something that makes someone believe something untrue

PERSUASIVE – describes something that makes you want to believe or do something

POST—TRUTH – the idea that beliefs are more important than facts and the truth

PREJUDICE – pre-judging another group of people without any factual information to go on

PROPAGANDA – information, that is sometimes false, used to try to influence people

SCEPTIC – someone who doubts that something is true

SOURCE – where something comes from

FURTHER INFORMATION

Here are some other books and websites that you can look at for more information on fake news, as well as related and important topics:

BOOKS

Super Social Media and Awesome Online Safety
by Clive Gifford (Wayland, 2017)

Who is Donald Trump?
by Julia Adams (Wayland, 2017)

Britain and the European Union
by Simon Adams (Franklin Watts, 2016)

WEBSITES

www.bbc.co.uk/newsround/38906931
Learn more about fake news and how to spot it.

www.snopes.com/category/facts/fake-news/
This website investigates news stories and presents evidence to confirm if they are true or false.

www.bbc.co.uk/cbbc/quizzes/real-or-fake-news-quiz
Try and see if you can spot the fake news articles in this quiz.

INDEX

MY OPINION
TRUMPS
YOUR FACTS
mrTrumphead.com